DAYBREAK
PROMISES
from PROVERBS

Titles in this series:

DAYBREAK
PROMISES

from PROVERBS

Compiled by DAVID M. CARDER

ZONDERVAN®

ZONDERVAN

DayBreak Promises from Proverbs
Copyright © 2012 by Zondervan
All rights reserved

This title is also available as a Zondervan ebook.
Visit www.zondervan.com/ebooks.

Requests for information should be addressed to:

Zondervan, *Grand Rapids, Michigan 49530*

Library of Congress Catalog Card Number 2012939817

Any Internet addresses (websites, blogs, etc.) and telephone numbers in this
book are offered as a resource. They are not intended in any way to be or
imply an endorsement by Zondervan, nor does Zondervan vouch for the
content of these sites and numbers for the life of this book.

Cover design: Jamie DeBruyn
Cover photography or illustration: istockphoto
Interior design: Nancy Wilson

Printed in the United States of America

12 13 14 15 16 17 18 /DPM/ 12 11 10 9 8 7 6 5 4 3 2 1

To my daughter Jeanna,
who encouraged me
to start this project.

CONTENTS

ADULTERY

PROVERBS 5:20–23

Why, my son, be intoxicated with another man's wife? Why embrace the bosom of a wayward woman? For your ways are in full view of the LORD, and he examines all your paths. The evil deeds of the wicked ensnare them; the cords of their sins hold them fast. For lack of discipline they will die, led astray by their own great folly.

PROVERBS 6:32–35

But a man who commits adultery has no sense; whoever does so destroys himself. Blows and disgrace are his lot, and his shame will never be wiped away. For jealousy arouses a husband's fury, and he will show no mercy when he takes revenge. He will not accept any compensation; he will refuse a bribe, however great it is.

PROVERBS 23:26–28

My son, give me your heart and let your eyes delight in my ways, for an adulterous woman is a deep pit, and a wayward wife is a narrow well. Like a bandit she lies in wait and multiplies the unfaithful among men.

PROVERBS 29:3

A man who loves wisdom brings joy to his father, but a companion of prostitutes squanders his wealth.

PROVERBS 30:20

"This is the way of an adulterous woman: She eats and wipes her mouth and says, 'I've done nothing wrong.'"

ALCOHOL

PROVERBS 20:1

Wine is a mocker and beer a brawler; whoever is led astray by them is not wise.

PROVERBS 21:17

Whoever loves pleasure will become poor; whoever loves wine and olive oil will never be rich.

PROVERBS 23:20–21

Do not join those who drink too much wine or gorge themselves on meat, for drunkards and gluttons become poor, and drowsiness clothes them in rags.

PROVERBS 23:29–35

Who has woe? Who has sorrow? Who has strife? Who has complaints? Who has needless bruises? Who has bloodshot eyes? Those who linger over wine, who go to sample bowls of mixed wine. Do not gaze at wine when it is red, when it sparkles in the cup, when it goes down smoothly! In the end it bites like a snake and poisons like a viper. Your eyes will see strange sights, and your mind will imagine confusing things. You will be like one sleeping on the high seas, lying on top of the rigging. "They hit me," you will say, "but I'm not hurt! They beat me, but I don't feel it! When will I wake up so I can find another drink?"

ANGER

PROVERBS 14:17

A quick-tempered person does foolish things, and the one who devises evil schemes is hated.

PROVERBS 15:1

A gentle answer turns away wrath, but a harsh word stirs up anger.

PROVERBS 15:18

A hot-tempered person stirs up conflict, but the one who is patient calms a quarrel.

PROVERBS 19:19

A hot-tempered person must pay the penalty; rescue them, and you will have to do it again.

PROVERBS 22:24–25

Do not make friends with a hot-tempered person, do not associate with one easily angered, or you may learn their ways and get yourself ensnared.

PROVERBS 25:23

Like a north wind that brings unexpected rain is a sly tongue — which provokes a horrified look.

PROVERBS 27:4

Anger is cruel and fury overwhelming, but who can stand before jealousy?

PROVERBS 29:11

Fools give full vent to their rage, but the wise bring calm in the end.

PROVERBS 29:22

An angry person stirs up conflict, and a hot-tempered person commits many sins.

PROVERBS 30:33

"For as churning cream produces butter, and as twisting the nose produces blood, so stirring up anger produces strife."

_____CORRECTION/DISCIPLINE_____

PROVERBS 3:11–12

My son, do not despise the LORD's discipline, and do not resent his rebuke, because the LORD disciplines those he loves, as a father the son he delights in.

PROVERBS 6:23

For this command is a lamp, this teaching is a light, and correction and instruction are the way to life.

PROVERBS 9:7

Whoever corrects a mocker invites insults; whoever rebukes the wicked incurs abuse.

PROVERBS 10:17

Whoever heeds discipline shows the way to life, but whoever ignores correction leads others astray.

PROVERBS 12:1

Whoever loves discipline loves knowledge, but whoever hates correction is stupid.

PROVERBS 13:18

Whoever disregards discipline comes to poverty and shame, but whoever heeds correction is honored.

PROVERBS 13:24

Whoever spares the rod hates their children, but the one who loves their children is careful to discipline them.

PROVERBS 15:10

Stern discipline awaits anyone who leaves the path; the one who hates correction will die.

PROVERBS 15:12

Mockers resent correction, so they avoid the wise.

PROVERBS 15:32

Those who disregard discipline despise themselves, but the one who heeds correction gains understanding.

PROVERBS 19:16

Whoever keeps commandments keeps their life, but whoever shows contempt for their ways will die.

PROVERBS 19:18

Discipline your children, for in that there is hope; do not be a willing party to their death.

PROVERBS 20:30

Blows and wounds scrub away evil, and beatings purge the inmost being.

PROVERBS 22:15

Folly is bound up in the heart of a child, but the rod of discipline will drive it far away.

PROVERBS 23:13–14

Do not withhold discipline from a child; if you punish them with the rod, they will not die. Punish them with the rod and save them from death.

PROVERBS 23:23

Buy the truth and do not sell it — wisdom, instruction and insight as well.

PROVERBS 29:15

A rod and a reprimand impart wisdom, but a child left undisciplined disgraces its mother.

PROVERBS 29:17

Discipline your children, and they will give you peace; they will bring you the delights you desire.

PROVERBS 29:19

Servants cannot be corrected by mere words; though they understand, they will not respond.

COUNSEL

PROVERBS 8:14

"Counsel and sound judgment are mine; I have insight, I have power."

PROVERBS 11:14

For lack of guidance a nation falls, but victory is won through many advisers.

PROVERBS 12:5

The plans of the righteous are just, but the advice of the wicked is deceitful.

PROVERBS 12:15

The way of fools seems right to them, but the wise listen to advice.

PROVERBS 12:20

Deceit is in the hearts of those who plot evil, but those who promote peace have joy.

PROVERBS 13:10

Where there is strife, there is pride, but wisdom is found in those who take advice.

PROVERBS 15:22

Plans fail for lack of counsel, but with many advisers they succeed.

PROVERBS 19:20

Listen to advice and accept discipline, and at the end you will be counted among the wise.

PROVERBS 20:18

Plans are established by seeking advice; so if you wage war, obtain guidance.

PROVERBS 21:30

There is no wisdom, no insight, no plan that can succeed against the LORD.

PROVERBS 27:9

Perfume and incense bring joy to the heart, and the pleasantness of a friend springs from their heartfelt advice.

DECEIT

PROVERBS 6:14

Who plots evil with deceit in his heart — he always stirs up conflict.

PROVERBS 12:5

The plans of the righteous are just, but the advice of the wicked is deceitful.

PROVERBS 12:20

Deceit is in the hearts of those who plot evil, but those who promote peace have joy.

PROVERBS 14:5

An honest witness does not deceive, but a false witness pours out lies.

PROVERBS 15:4

The soothing tongue is a tree of life, but a perverse tongue crushes the spirit.

PROVERBS 17:20

One whose heart is corrupt does not prosper; one whose tongue is perverse falls into trouble.

PROVERBS 24:28

Do not testify against your neighbor without cause — would you use your lips to mislead?

PROVERBS 26:19

Is one who deceives their neighbor and says, "I was only joking!"

PROVERBS 26:24

Enemies disguise themselves with their lips, but in their hearts they harbor deceit.

_____DESIRES_____

PROVERBS 8:11

"For wisdom is more precious than rubies, and nothing you desire can compare with her."

PROVERBS 10:24

What the wicked dread will overtake them; what the righteous desire will be granted.

PROVERBS 11:23

The desire of the righteous ends only in good, but the hope of the wicked only in wrath.

PROVERBS 13:2

From the fruit of their lips people enjoy good things, but the unfaithful have an appetite for violence.

PROVERBS 13:4

A sluggard's appetite is never filled, but the desires of the diligent are fully satisfied.

PROVERBS 13:12

Hope deferred makes the heart sick, but a longing fulfilled is a tree of life.

PROVERBS 13:19

A longing fulfilled is sweet to the soul, but fools detest turning from evil.

PROVERBS 21:25–26

The craving of a sluggard will be the death of him, because his hands refuse to work. All day long he craves for more, but the righteous give without sparing.

PROVERBS 24:1

Do not envy the wicked, do not desire their company.

DILIGENCE

PROVERBS 10:4

Lazy hands make for poverty, but diligent hands bring wealth.

PROVERBS 12:11

Those who work their land will have abundant food, but those who chase fantasies have no sense.

PROVERBS 12:14

From the fruit of their lips people are filled with good things, and the work of their hands brings them reward.

PROVERBS 12:24

Diligent hands will rule, but laziness ends in forced labor.

PROVERBS 13:4

A sluggard's appetite is never filled, but the desires of the diligent are fully satisfied.

PROVERBS 13:11

Dishonest money dwindles away, but whoever gathers money little by little makes it grow.

PROVERBS 14:23

All hard work brings a profit, but mere talk leads only to poverty.

PROVERBS 21:5

The plans of the diligent lead to profit as surely as haste leads to poverty.

PROVERBS 24:10

If you falter in a time of trouble, how small is your strength!

PROVERBS 28:20

A faithful person will be richly blessed, but one eager to get rich will not go unpunished.

_____DISCERNMENT_____

PROVERBS 1:5

Let the wise listen and add to their learning, and let the discerning get guidance.

PROVERBS 2:11

Discretion will protect you, and understanding will guard you.

PROVERBS 3:21–24

My son, do not let wisdom and understanding out of your sight, preserve sound judgment and discretion; they will be life for you, an ornament to grace your neck. Then you will go on your way in safety, and your foot will not stumble. When you lie down, you will not be afraid; when you lie down, your sleep will be sweet.

PROVERBS 11:12

Whoever derides their neighbor has no sense, but the one who has understanding holds their tongue.

PROVERBS 16:21

The wise in heart are called discerning, and gracious words promote instruction.

PROVERBS 19:25

Flog a mocker, and the simple will learn prudence; rebuke the discerning, and they will gain knowledge.

PROVERBS 28:7

A discerning son heeds instruction, but a companion of gluttons disgraces his father.

PROVERBS 28:11

The rich are wise in their own eyes; one who is poor and discerning sees how deluded they are.

EMOTIONS

PROVERBS 1:33

"But whoever listens to me will live in safety and be at ease, without fear of harm."

PROVERBS 12:25

Anxiety weighs down the heart, but a kind word cheers it up.

PROVERBS 13:12

Hope deferred makes the heart sick, but a longing fulfilled is a tree of life.

PROVERBS 14:10

Each heart knows its own bitterness, and no one else can share its joy.

PROVERBS 14:13

Even in laughter the heart may ache, and rejoicing may end in grief.

PROVERBS 14:30

A heart at peace gives life to the body, but envy rots the bones.

PROVERBS 15:13

A happy heart makes the face cheerful, but heartache crushes the spirit.

PROVERBS 15:30

Light in a messenger's eyes brings joy to the heart, and good news gives health to the bones.

PROVERBS 18:14

The human spirit can endure in sickness, but a crushed spirit who can bear?

PROVERBS 24:19

Do not fret because of evildoers or be envious of the wicked.

PROVERBS 25:20

Like one who takes away a garment on a cold day, or like vinegar poured on a wound, is one who sings songs to a heavy heart.

_____ETHICS, BUSINESS_____

PROVERBS 6:1–5

My son, if you have put up security for your neighbor, if you have shaken hands in pledge for a stranger, you have been trapped by what you said, ensnared by the words of your mouth. So do this, my son, to free yourself, since you have fallen into your neighbor's hands: Go — to the point of exhaustion — and give your neighbor no rest! Allow no sleep to your eyes, no slumber to your eyelids. Free yourself, like a gazelle from the hand of the hunter, like a bird from the snare of the fowler.

PROVERBS 11:1

The LORD detests dishonest scales, but accurate weights find favor with him.

PROVERBS 11:24–26

One person gives freely, yet gains even more; another withholds unduly, but comes to poverty. A generous person will prosper; whoever refreshes others will be refreshed. People curse the one who hoards grain, but they pray God's blessing on the one who is willing to sell.

PROVERBS 25:8

Do not bring hastily to court, for what will you do in the end if your neighbor puts you to shame?

PROVERBS 28:8

Whoever increases wealth by taking interest or profit from the poor amasses it for another, who will be kind to the poor.

_____FAMILY_____

PROVERBS 11:29

Whoever brings ruin on their family will inherit only wind, and the fool will be servant to the wise.

PROVERBS 13:22

A good person leaves an inheritance for their children's children, but a sinner's wealth is stored up for the righteous.

PROVERBS 15:27

The greedy bring ruin to their households, but the one who hates bribes will live.

PROVERBS 17:6

Children's children are a crown to the aged, and parents are the pride of their children.

PROVERBS 17:17

A friend loves at all times, and a brother is born for a time of adversity.

PROVERBS 18:19

A brother wronged is more unyielding than a fortified city; disputes are like the barred gates of a citadel.

PROVERBS 27:10

Do not forsake your friend or a friend of your family, and do not go to your relative's house when disaster strikes you — better a neighbor nearby than a relative far away.

PROVERBS 31:15

She [a wife] gets up while it is still night; she provides food for her family and portions for her female servants.

_____FAVOR_____

PROVERBS 8:35

"For those who find me find life and receive favor from the LORD."

PROVERBS 12:2

Good people obtain favor from the LORD, but he condemns those who devise wicked schemes.

PROVERBS 13:15

Good judgment wins favor, but the way of the unfaithful leads to their destruction.

PROVERBS 16:13

Kings take pleasure in honest lips; they value the one who speaks what is right.

PROVERBS 19:6

Many curry favor with a ruler, and everyone is the friend of one who gives gifts.

PROVERBS 19:12

A king's rage is like the roar of a lion, but his favor is like dew on the grass.

PROVERBS 21:3

To do what is right and just is more acceptable to the LORD than sacrifice.

PROVERBS 22:1

A good name is more desirable than great riches; to be esteemed is better than silver or gold.

PROVERBS 28:23

Whoever rebukes a person will in the end gain favor rather than one who has a flattering tongue.

PROVERBS 29:23

Pride brings a person low, but the lowly in spirit gain honor.

_____FEAR OF THE LORD_____

PROVERBS 8:13

"To fear the LORD is to hate evil; I hate pride and arrogance, evil behavior and perverse speech."

PROVERBS 9:10

The fear of the LORD is the beginning of wisdom, and knowledge of the Holy One is understanding.

PROVERBS 10:27

The fear of the LORD adds length to life, but the years of the wicked are cut short.

PROVERBS 14:26–27

Whoever fears the LORD has a secure fortress, and for their children it will be a refuge. The fear of the LORD is a fountain of life, turning a person from the snares of death.

PROVERBS 15:16

Better a little with the fear of the LORD than great wealth with turmoil.

PROVERBS 15:33

Wisdom's instruction is to fear the LORD, and humility comes before honor.

PROVERBS 16:6

Through love and faithfulness sin is atoned for; through the fear of the LORD evil is avoided.

PROVERBS 19:23

The fear of the LORD leads to life; then one rests content, untouched by trouble.

PROVERBS 22:4

Humility is the fear of the LORD; its wages are riches and honor and life.

FOOLS

PROVERBS 1:32

"For the waywardness of the simple will kill them, and the complacency of fools will destroy them."

PROVERBS 10:8

The wise in heart accept commands, but a chattering fool comes to ruin.

PROVERBS 10:14

The wise store up knowledge, but the mouth of a fool invites ruin.

PROVERBS 10:18

Whoever conceals hatred with lying lips and spreads slander is a fool.

PROVERBS 12:15–16

The way of fools seems right to them, but the wise listen to advice. Fools show their annoyance at once, but the prudent overlook an insult.

PROVERBS 12:23

The prudent keep their knowledge to themselves, but a fool's heart blurts out folly.

PROVERBS 14:9

Fools mock at making amends for sin, but goodwill is found among the upright.

PROVERBS 15:2

The tongue of the wise adorns knowledge, but the mouth of the fool gushes folly.

PROVERBS 15:5

A fool spurns a parent's discipline, but whoever heeds correction shows prudence.

PROVERBS 15:20

A wise son brings joy to his father, but a foolish man despises his mother.

PROVERBS 15:21

Folly brings joy to one who has no sense, but whoever has understanding keeps a straight course.

PROVERBS 17:12

Better to meet a bear robbed of her cubs than a fool bent on folly.

PROVERBS 17:28

Even fools are thought wise if they keep silent, and discerning if they hold their tongues.

PROVERBS 18:2

Fools find no pleasure in understanding but delight in airing their own opinions.

PROVERBS 18:6–7

The lips of fools bring them strife, and their mouths invite a beating. The mouths of fools are their undoing, and their lips are a snare to their very lives.

PROVERBS 19:3

A person's own folly leads to their ruin, yet their heart rages against the LORD.

PROVERBS 20:3

It is to one's honor to avoid strife, but every fool is quick to quarrel.

PROVERBS 23:9

Do not speak to fools, for they will scorn your prudent words.

PROVERBS 26:1–12

Like snow in summer or rain in harvest, honor is not fitting for a fool. Like a fluttering sparrow or a darting swallow, an undeserved curse does not come to rest. A whip for the horse, a bridle for the donkey, and a rod for the backs of fools! Do not answer a fool according to his folly, or you yourself will be just like him. Answer a fool according to his folly, or he will be wise in his own eyes. Sending a message by the hands of a fool is like cutting off one's feet or drinking poison. Like the useless legs of one who is lame is a proverb in the mouth of a fool. Like tying a stone in a sling is the giving of honor to a fool. Like a thornbush in a drunkard's hand is a proverb in the mouth of a fool. Like an archer who wounds at random is one who hires a fool or any passer-by. As a dog returns to its vomit, so fools repeat their folly. Do you see a person wise in their own eyes? There is more hope for a fool than for them.

PROVERBS 27:3

Stone is heavy and sand a burden, but a fool's provocation is heavier than both.

PROVERBS 27:22

Though you grind a fool in a mortar, grinding them like grain with a pestle, you will not remove their folly from them.

PROVERBS 28:26

Those who trust in themselves are fools, but those who walk in wisdom are kept safe.

PROVERBS 29:9

If a wise person goes to court with a fool, the fool rages and scoffs, and there is no peace.

PROVERBS 29:11

Fools give full vent to their rage, but the wise bring calm in the end.

PROVERBS 30:32

"If you play the fool and exalt yourself, or if you plan evil, clap your hand over your mouth!"

_____FRIENDS/COMPANIONS_____

PROVERBS 16:28

A perverse person stirs up conflict, and a gossip separates close friends.

PROVERBS 17:9

Whoever would foster love covers over an offense, but whoever repeats the matter separates close friends.

PROVERBS 17:17

A friend loves at all times, and a brother is born for a time of adversity.

PROVERBS 22:11

One who loves a pure heart and who speaks with grace will have the king for a friend.

PROVERBS 22:24

Do not make friends with a hot-tempered person, do not associate with one easily angered.

PROVERBS 27:6

Wounds from a friend can be trusted, but an enemy multiplies kisses.

PROVERBS 27:9b–10

And the pleasantness of a friend springs from their heartfelt advice. Do not forsake your friend or a friend of your family, and do not go to your relative's house when disaster strikes you — better a neighbor nearby than a relative far away.

GOVERNMENT

PROVERBS 8:16

"By me princes govern, and nobles — all who rule on earth."

PROVERBS 11:10–11

When the righteous prosper, the city rejoices; when the wicked perish, there are shouts of joy. Through the blessing of the upright a city is exalted, but by the mouth of the wicked it is destroyed.

PROVERBS 25:15

Through patience a ruler can be persuaded, and a gentle tongue can break a bone.

PROVERBS 28:2–3

When a country is rebellious, it has many rulers, but a ruler with discernment and knowledge maintains order. A ruler who oppresses the poor is like a driving rain that leaves no crops.

PROVERBS 28:15–16

Like a roaring lion or a charging bear is a wicked ruler over a helpless people. A tyrannical ruler practices extortion, but one who hates ill-gotten gain will enjoy a long reign.

PROVERBS 29:2

When the righteous thrive, the people rejoice; when the wicked rule, the people groan.

PROVERBS 29:12

If a ruler listens to lies, all his officials become wicked.

PROVERBS 29:26

Many seek an audience with a ruler, but it is from the LORD that one gets justice.

GREED/STINGINESS

PROVERBS 10:2

Ill-gotten treasures have no lasting value, but righteousness delivers from death.

PROVERBS 13:11

Dishonest money dwindles away, but whoever gathers money little by little makes it grow.

PROVERBS 15:27

The greedy bring ruin to their households, but the one who hates bribes will live.

PROVERBS 20:17

Food gained by fraud tastes sweet, but one ends up with a mouth full of gravel.

PROVERBS 21:6

A fortune made by a lying tongue is a fleeting vapor and a deadly snare.

PROVERBS 21:20

The wise store up choice food and olive oil, but fools gulp theirs down.

PROVERBS 22:16

One who oppresses the poor to increase his wealth and one who gives gifts to the rich — both come to poverty.

PROVERBS 28:8

Whoever increases wealth by taking interest or profit from the poor amasses it for another, who will be kind to the poor.

PROVERBS 28:20

A faithful person will be richly blessed, but one eager to get rich will not go unpunished.

PROVERBS 28:22

The stingy are eager to get rich and are unaware that poverty awaits them.

_____GUIDANCE/PATHS_____

PROVERBS 3:5–6

Trust in the LORD with all your heart and lean not on your own understanding; in all your ways submit to him, and he will make your paths straight.

PROVERBS 4:11

I instruct you in the way of wisdom and lead you along straight paths.

PROVERBS 4:26–27

Give careful thought to the paths for your feet and be steadfast in all your ways. Do not turn to the right or the left; keep your foot from evil.

PROVERBS 5:21

For your ways are in full view of the LORD, and he examines all your paths.

PROVERBS 10:9

Whoever walks in integrity walks securely, but whoever takes crooked paths will be found out.

PROVERBS 12:28

In the way of righteousness there is life; along that path is immortality.

PROVERBS 14:12

There is a way that appears to be right, but in the end it leads to death.

PROVERBS 15:24

The path of life leads upward for the prudent to keep them from going down to the realm of the dead.

PROVERBS 16:1

To humans belong the plans of the heart, but from the LORD comes the proper answer of the tongue.

PROVERBS 16:3

Commit to the LORD whatever you do, and he will establish your plans.

PROVERBS 16:7

When the LORD takes pleasure in anyone's way, he causes their enemies to make peace with them.

PROVERBS 16:9

In their hearts humans plan their course, but the LORD establishes their steps.

PROVERBS 16:17

The highway of the upright avoids evil; those who guard their ways preserve their lives.

PROVERBS 16:33

The lot is cast into the lap, but its every decision is from the LORD.

PROVERBS 18:18

Casting the lot settles disputes and keeps strong opponents apart.

PROVERBS 19:21

Many are the plans in a person's heart, but it is the LORD's purpose that prevails.

PROVERBS 20:24

A person's steps are directed by the LORD. How then can anyone understand their own way?

PROVERBS 21:1

In the LORD's hand the king's heart is a stream of water that he channels toward all who please him.

PROVERBS 21:16

Whoever strays from the path of prudence comes to rest in the company of the dead.

HEALTH

PROVERBS 3:1–2

My son, do not forget my teaching, but keep my commands in your heart, for they will prolong your life many years and bring you peace and prosperity.

PROVERBS 3:7–8

Do not be wise in your own eyes; fear the LORD and shun evil. This will bring health to your body and nourishment to your bones.

PROVERBS 3:13–18

Blessed are those who find wisdom, those who gain understanding, for she is more profitable than silver and yields better returns than gold. She is more precious than rubies;

nothing you desire can compare with her. Long life is in her right hand; in her left hand are riches and honor. Her ways are pleasant ways, and all her paths are peace. She is a tree of life to those who take hold of her; those who hold her fast will be blessed.

PROVERBS 12:18

The words of the reckless pierce like swords, but the tongue of the wise brings healing.

PROVERBS 15:30

Light in a messenger's eyes brings joy to the heart, and good news gives health to the bones.

_____HEART_____

PROVERBS 4:23

Above all else, guard your heart, for everything you do flows from it.

PROVERBS 10:8

The wise in heart accept commands, but a chattering fool comes to ruin.

PROVERBS 16:23

The hearts of the wise make their mouths prudent, and their lips promote instruction.

PROVERBS 17:3

The crucible for silver and the furnace for gold, but the LORD tests the heart.

PROVERBS 17:20

One whose heart is corrupt does not prosper; one whose tongue is perverse falls into trouble.

PROVERBS 23:17

Do not let your heart envy sinners, but always be zealous for the fear of the LORD.

PROVERBS 23:19

Listen, my son, and be wise, and set your heart on the right path.

PROVERBS 24:32

I applied my heart to what I observed and learned a lesson from what I saw.

PROVERBS 25:20

Like one who takes away a garment on a cold day, or like vinegar poured on a wound, is one who sings songs to a heavy heart.

PROVERBS 27:19

As water reflects the face, so one's life reflects the heart.

PROVERBS 28:14

Blessed is the one who always trembles before God, but whoever hardens their heart falls into trouble.

HUMILITY/PRIDE

PROVERBS 11:2

When pride comes, then comes disgrace, but with humility comes wisdom.

PROVERBS 15:25

The LORD tears down the house of the proud, but he sets the widow's boundary stones in place.

PROVERBS 15:33

Wisdom's instruction is to fear the LORD, and humility comes before honor.

PROVERBS 16:5

The LORD detests all the proud of heart. Be sure of this: They will not go unpunished.

PROVERBS 16:18–19

Pride goes before destruction, a haughty spirit before a fall. Better to be lowly in spirit along with the oppressed than to share plunder with the proud.

PROVERBS 18:12

Before a downfall the heart is haughty, but humility comes before honor.

PROVERBS 22:4

Humility is the fear of the LORD; its wages are riches and honor and life.

PROVERBS 25:6–7

Do not exalt yourself in the king's presence, and do not claim a place among his great men; it is better for him to say to you, "Come up here," than for him to humiliate you before his nobles. What you have seen with your eyes.

PROVERBS 29:23

Pride brings a person low, but the lowly in spirit gain honor.

_____JOY_____

PROVERBS 10:28a

The prospect of the righteous is joy.

PROVERBS 11:10

When the righteous prosper, the city rejoices; when the wicked perish, there are shouts of joy.

PROVERBS 12:20

Deceit is in the hearts of those who plot evil, but those who promote peace have joy.

PROVERBS 14:10

Each heart knows its own bitterness, and no one else can share its joy.

PROVERBS 14:13

Even in laughter the heart may ache, and rejoicing may end in grief.

PROVERBS 15:20

A wise son brings joy to his father, but a foolish man despises his mother.

PROVERBS 15:23

A person finds joy in giving an apt reply — and how good is a timely word!

PROVERBS 21:15

When justice is done, it brings joy to the righteous but terror to evildoers.

PROVERBS 23:24

The father of a righteous child has great joy; a man who fathers a wise son rejoices in him.

PROVERBS 27:9

Perfume and incense bring joy to the heart, and the pleasantness of a friend springs from their heartfelt advice.

_____JUDGMENT_____

PROVERBS 3:25–26

Have no fear of sudden disaster or of the ruin that overtakes the wicked, for the LORD will be at your side and will keep your foot from being snared.

PROVERBS 17:20

One whose heart is corrupt does not prosper; one whose tongue is perverse falls into trouble.

PROVERBS 20:20

If someone curses their father or mother, their lamp will be snuffed out in pitch darkness.

PROVERBS 22:14

The mouth of an adulterous woman is a deep pit; a man who is under the LORD's wrath falls into it.

PROVERBS 26:27

Whoever digs a pit will fall into it; if someone rolls a stone, it will roll back on them.

PROVERBS 28:10

Whoever leads the upright along an evil path will fall into their own trap, but the blameless will receive a good inheritance.

PROVERBS 28:14

Blessed is the one who always trembles before God, but whoever hardens their heart falls into trouble.

PROVERBS 28:18

The one whose walk is blameless is kept safe, but the one whose ways are perverse will fall into the pit.

PROVERBS 29:1

Whoever remains stiff-necked after many rebukes will suddenly be destroyed — without remedy.

JUSTICE

PROVERBS 17:15

Acquitting the guilty and condemning the innocent — the LORD detests them both.

PROVERBS 18:5

It is not good to be partial to the wicked and so deprive the innocent of justice.

PROVERBS 24:23–26

These also are sayings of the wise: To show partiality in judging is not good: Whoever says to the guilty, "You are innocent," will be cursed by peoples and denounced by nations. But it will go well with those who convict the guilty, and rich blessing will come on them. An honest answer is like a kiss on the lips.

PROVERBS 28:21

To show partiality is not good — yet a person will do wrong for a piece of bread.

PROVERBS 29:7

The righteous care about justice for the poor, but the wicked have no such concern.

PROVERBS 29:14

If a king judges the poor with fairness, his throne will be established forever.

PROVERBS 29:26

Many seek an audience with a ruler, but it is from the LORD that one gets justice.

PROVERBS 31:8–9

Speak up for those who cannot speak for themselves, for the rights of all who are destitute. Speak up and judge fairly; defend the rights of the poor and needy.

KNOWLEDGE

PROVERBS 1:7

The fear of the LORD is the beginning of knowledge, but fools despise wisdom and instruction.

PROVERBS 10:14

The wise store up knowledge, but the mouth of a fool invites ruin.

PROVERBS 12:1

Whoever loves discipline loves knowledge, but whoever hates correction is stupid.

PROVERBS 12:23

The prudent keep their knowledge to themselves, but a fool's heart blurts out folly.

PROVERBS 15:7

The lips of the wise spread knowledge, but the hearts of fools are not upright.

PROVERBS 15:14

The discerning heart seeks knowledge, but the mouth of a fool feeds on folly.

PROVERBS 17:27

The one who has knowledge uses words with restraint, and whoever has understanding is even-tempered.

PROVERBS 18:15

The heart of the discerning acquires knowledge, for the ears of the wise seek it out.

PROVERBS 19:2

Desire without knowledge is not good — how much more will hasty feet miss the way!

PROVERBS 19:25

Flog a mocker, and the simple will learn prudence; rebuke the discerning, and they will gain knowledge.

PROVERBS 19:27

Stop listening to instruction, my son, and you will stray from the words of knowledge.

PROVERBS 20:15

Gold there is, and rubies in abundance, but lips that speak knowledge are a rare jewel.

_____LAZINESS_____

PROVERBS 10:26

As vinegar to the teeth and smoke to the eyes, so are sluggards to those who send them.

PROVERBS 12:27

The lazy do not roast any game, but the diligent feed on the riches of the hunt.

PROVERBS 15:19

The way of the sluggard is blocked with thorns, but the path of the upright is a highway.

PROVERBS 18:9

One who is slack in his work is brother to one who destroys.

PROVERBS 19:15

Laziness brings on deep sleep, and the shiftless go hungry.

PROVERBS 20:4

Sluggards do not plow in season; so at harvest time they look but find nothing.

PROVERBS 20:13

Do not love sleep or you will grow poor; stay awake and you will have food to spare.

PROVERBS 21:25–26

The craving of a sluggard will be the death of him, because his hands refuse to work. All day long he craves for more, but the righteous give without sparing.

PROVERBS 26:13–16

A sluggard says, "There's a lion in the road, a fierce lion roaming the streets!" As a door turns on its hinges, so a sluggard turns on his bed. A sluggard buries his hand in the dish; he is too lazy to bring it back to his mouth. A sluggard is wiser in his own eyes than seven people who answer discreetly.

LISTENING

PROVERBS 1:5

Let the wise listen and add to their learning, and let the discerning get guidance.

PROVERBS 1:33

"But whoever listens to me will live in safety and be at ease, without fear of harm."

PROVERBS 4:10

Listen, my son, accept what I say, and the years of your life will be many.

PROVERBS 15:29

The LORD is far from the wicked, but he hears the prayer of the righteous.

PROVERBS 15:31

Whoever heeds life-giving correction will be at home among the wise.

PROVERBS 17:4

A wicked person listens to deceitful lips; a liar pays attention to a destructive tongue.

PROVERBS 18:13

To answer before listening — that is folly and shame.

PROVERBS 18:17

In a lawsuit the first to speak seems right, until someone comes forward and cross-examines.

PROVERBS 19:20

Listen to advice and accept discipline, and at the end you will be counted among the wise.

PROVERBS 25:12

Like an earring of gold or an ornament of fine gold is the rebuke of a wise judge to a listening ear.

_____LOVE_____

PROVERBS 3:3

Let love and faithfulness never leave you; bind them around your neck, write them on the tablet of your heart.

PROVERBS 10:12

Hatred stirs up conflict, but love covers over all wrongs.

PROVERBS 14:22

Do not those who plot evil go astray? But those who plan what is good find love and faithfulness.

PROVERBS 16:6

Through love and faithfulness sin is atoned for; through the fear of the LORD evil is avoided.

PROVERBS 17:9

Whoever would foster love covers over an offense, but whoever repeats the matter separates close friends.

PROVERBS 19:22

What a person desires is unfailing love; better to be poor than a liar.

PROVERBS 20:6

Many claim to have unfailing love, but a faithful person who can find?

PROVERBS 20:28

Love and faithfulness keep a king safe; through love his throne is made secure.

PROVERBS 21:21

Whoever pursues righteousness and love finds life, prosperity and honor.

PROVERBS 27:5

Better is open rebuke than hidden love.

_____LYING_____

PROVERBS 10:18

Whoever conceals hatred with lying lips and spreads slander is a fool.

PROVERBS 12:17

An honest witness tells the truth, but a false witness tells lies.

PROVERBS 12:22

The LORD detests lying lips, but he delights in people who are trustworthy.

PROVERBS 14:5

An honest witness does not deceive, but a false witness pours out lies.

PROVERBS 14:25

A truthful witness saves lives, but a false witness is deceitful.

PROVERBS 17:4

A wicked person listens to deceitful lips; a liar pays attention to a destructive tongue.

PROVERBS 19:9

A false witness will not go unpunished, and whoever pours out lies will perish.

PROVERBS 19:22

What a person desires is unfailing love; better to be poor than a liar.

PROVERBS 26:28

A lying tongue hates those it hurts, and a flattering mouth works ruin.

PROVERBS 29:12

If a ruler listens to lies, all his officials become wicked.

PROVERBS 30:7–8

"Two things I ask of you, LORD; do not refuse me before I die: Keep falsehood and lies far from me; give me neither poverty nor riches, but give me only my daily bread."

———————————MEN———————————

PROVERBS 3:35

The wise inherit honor, but fools get only shame.

PROVERBS 5:22–23

The evil deeds of the wicked ensnare them; the cords of their sins hold them fast. For lack of discipline they will die, led astray by their own great folly.

PROVERBS 9:8–9

Do not rebuke mockers or they will hate you; rebuke the wise and they will love you. Instruct the wise and they will be wiser still; teach the righteous and they will add to their learning.

PROVERBS 9:12

If you are wise, your wisdom will reward you; if you are a mocker, you alone will suffer.

PROVERBS 10:8

The wise in heart accept commands, but a chattering fool comes to ruin.

PROVERBS 10:24

What the wicked dread will overtake them; what the righteous desire will be granted.

PROVERBS 12:10

The righteous care for the needs of their animals, but the kindest acts of the wicked are cruel.

PROVERBS 13:14

The teaching of the wise is a fountain of life, turning a person from the snares of death.

PROVERBS 13:20

Walk with the wise and become wise, for a companion of fools suffers harm.

PROVERBS 15:24

The path of life leads upward for the prudent to keep them from going down to the realm of the dead.

PROVERBS 15:31

Whoever heeds life-giving correction will be at home among the wise.

PROVERBS 17:11

Evildoers foster rebellion against God; the messenger of death will be sent against them.

PROVERBS 17:13

Evil will never leave the house of one who pays back evil for good.

PROVERBS 18:3

When wickedness comes, so does contempt, and with shame comes reproach.

PROVERBS 18:15

The heart of the discerning acquires knowledge, for the ears of the wise seek it out.

PROVERBS 19:20

Listen to advice and accept discipline, and at the end you will be counted among the wise.

PROVERBS 21:7

The violence of the wicked will drag them away, for they refuse to do what is right.

PROVERBS 22:8

Whoever sows injustice reaps calamity, and the rod they wield in fury will be broken.

PROVERBS 24:5

The wise prevail through great power, and those who have knowledge muster their strength.

PROVERBS 24:20

For the evildoer has no future hope, and the lamp of the wicked will be snuffed out.

PROVERBS 28:28

When the wicked rise to power, people go into hiding; but when the wicked perish, the righteous thrive.

_____MOCKER_____

PROVERBS 1:22

"How long will you who are simple love your simple ways? How long will mockers delight in mockery and fools hate knowledge?"

PROVERBS 3:34

He [the LORD] mocks proud mockers but shows favor to the humble and oppressed.

PROVERBS 9:7–8

Whoever corrects a mocker invites insults; whoever rebukes the wicked incurs abuse. Do not rebuke mockers or they will hate you; rebuke the wise and they will love you.

PROVERBS 9:12

If you are wise, your wisdom will reward you; if you are a mocker, you alone will suffer.

PROVERBS 13:1

A wise son heeds his father's instruction, but a mocker does not respond to rebukes.

PROVERBS 14:6

The mocker seeks wisdom and finds none, but knowledge comes easily to the discerning.

PROVERBS 14:9

Fools mock at making amends for sin, but goodwill is found among the upright.

PROVERBS 15:12

Mockers resent correction, so they avoid the wise.

PROVERBS 21:11

When a mocker is punished, the simple gain wisdom; by paying attention to the wise they get knowledge.

PROVERBS 22:10

Drive out the mocker, and out goes strife; quarrels and insults are ended.

MOTIVES

PROVERBS 5:21

For your ways are in full view of the LORD, and he examines all your paths.

PROVERBS 15:3

The eyes of the LORD are everywhere, keeping watch on the wicked and the good.

PROVERBS 16:2

All a person's ways seem pure to them, but motives are weighed by the LORD.

PROVERBS 17:3

The crucible for silver and the furnace for gold, but the LORD tests the heart.

PROVERBS 20:5

The purposes of a person's heart are deep waters, but one who has insight draws them out.

PROVERBS 20:27

The human spirit is the lamp of the LORD that sheds light on one's inmost being.

PROVERBS 21:2

A person may think their own ways are right, but the LORD weighs the heart.

PROVERBS 24:12

If you say, "But we knew nothing about this," does not he who weighs the heart perceive it? Does not he who guards your life know it? Will he not repay everyone according to what they have done?

_____NEIGHBORS_____

PROVERBS 3:28–29

Do not say to your neighbor, "Come back tomorrow and I'll give it to you" — when you already have it with you. Do not plot harm against your neighbor, who lives trustfully near you.

PROVERBS 24:28

Do not testify against your neighbor without cause — would you use your lips to mislead?

PROVERBS 25:9–10

If you take your neighbor to court, do not betray another's confidence, or the one who hears it may shame you and the charge against you will stand.

PROVERBS 25:17–18

Seldom set foot in your neighbor's house — too much of you, and they will hate you. Like a club or a sword or a sharp arrow is one who gives false testimony against a neighbor.

PROVERBS 26:18–19

Like a maniac shooting flaming arrows of death is one who deceives their neighbor and says, "I was only joking!"

PROVERBS 27:10

Do not forsake your friend or a friend of your family, and do not go to your relative's house when disaster strikes you — better a neighbor nearby than a relative far away.

OBEDIENCE

PROVERBS 7:1–2

My son, keep my words and store up my commands within you. Keep my commands and you will live; guard my teachings as the apple of your eye.

PROVERBS 8:32

"Now then, my children, listen to me; blessed are those who keep my ways."

PROVERBS 16:20

Whoever gives heed to instruction prospers, and blessed is the one who trusts in the LORD.

PROVERBS 19:16

Whoever keeps commandments keeps their life, but whoever shows contempt for their ways will die.

PROVERBS 22:17–18

Pay attention and turn your ear to the sayings of the wise; apply your heart to what I teach, for it is pleasing when you keep them in your heart and have all of them ready on your lips.

PROVERBS 28:4

Those who forsake instruction praise the wicked, but those who heed it resist them.

PROVERBS 28:9

If anyone turns a deaf ear to my instruction, even their prayers are detestable.

PROVERBS 29:18

Where there is no revelation, people cast off restraint; but blessed is the one who heeds wisdom's instruction.

_____PARENT/CHILD_____

PROVERBS 13:24

Whoever spares the rod hates their children, but the one who loves their children is careful to discipline them.

PROVERBS 15:5

A fool spurns a parent's discipline, but whoever heeds correction shows prudence.

PROVERBS 17:6

Children's children are a crown to the aged, and parents are the pride of their children.

PROVERBS 19:18

Discipline your children, for in that there is hope; do not be a willing party to their death.

PROVERBS 20:20

If someone curses their father or mother, their lamp will be snuffed out in pitch darkness.

PROVERBS 22:6

Start children off on the way they should go, and even when they are old they will not turn from it.

PROVERBS 29:3

A man who loves wisdom brings joy to his father, but a companion of prostitutes squanders his wealth.

PROVERBS 29:15

A rod and a reprimand impart wisdom, but a child left undisciplined disgraces its mother.

PROVERBS 29:17

Discipline your children, and they will give you peace; they will bring you the delights you desire.

_____PATIENCE_____

PROVERBS 14:29

Whoever is patient has great understanding, but one who is quick-tempered displays folly.

PROVERBS 15:18

A hot-tempered person stirs up conflict, but the one who is patient calms a quarrel.

PROVERBS 16:32

Better a patient person than a warrior, one with self-control than one who takes a city.

PROVERBS 17:27

The one who has knowledge uses words with restraint, and whoever has understanding is even-tempered.

PROVERBS 19:11

A person's wisdom yields patience; it is to one's glory to overlook an offense.

PROVERBS 25:15

Through patience a ruler can be persuaded, and a gentle tongue can break a bone.

_____PERVERSION_____

PROVERBS 3:32

For the LORD detests the perverse but takes the upright into his confidence.

PROVERBS 10:31–32

From the mouth of the righteous comes the fruit of wisdom, but a perverse tongue will be silenced. The lips of the righteous know what finds favor, but the mouth of the wicked only what is perverse.

PROVERBS 11:20

The LORD detests those whose hearts are perverse, but he delights in those whose ways are blameless.

PROVERBS 12:8

A person is praised according to their prudence, and one with a warped mind is despised.

PROVERBS 16:30

Whoever winks with their eye is plotting perversity; whoever purses their lips is bent on evil.

PROVERBS 17:20

One whose heart is corrupt does not prosper; one whose tongue is perverse falls into trouble.

PROVERBS 19:1

Better the poor whose walk is blameless than a fool whose lips are perverse.

PROVERBS 28:6

Better the poor whose walk is blameless than the rich whose ways are perverse.

PROVERBS 28:18

The one whose walk is blameless is kept safe, but the one whose ways are perverse will fall into the pit.

PLANS

PROVERBS 12:20

Deceit is in the hearts of those who plot evil, but those who promote peace have joy.

PROVERBS 14:8

The wisdom of the prudent is to give thought to their ways, but the folly of fools is deception.

PROVERBS 14:15

The simple believe anything, but the prudent give thought to their steps.

PROVERBS 14:22

Do not those who plot evil go astray? But those who plan what is good find love and faithfulness.

PROVERBS 15:22

Plans fail for lack of counsel, but with many advisers they succeed.

PROVERBS 16:1

To humans belong the plans of the heart, but from the LORD comes the proper answer of the tongue.

PROVERBS 16:3

Commit to the LORD whatever you do, and he will establish your plans.

PROVERBS 16:9

In their hearts humans plan their course, but the LORD establishes their steps.

PROVERBS 21:29–30

The wicked put up a bold front, but the upright give thought to their ways. There is no wisdom, no insight, no plan that can succeed against the LORD.

———————————————POOR———————————————

PROVERBS 10:4

Lazy hands make for poverty, but diligent hands bring wealth.

PROVERBS 14:31

Whoever oppresses the poor shows contempt for their Maker, but whoever is kind to the needy honors God.

PROVERBS 16:8

Better a little with righteousness than much gain with injustice.

PROVERBS 17:5

Whoever mocks the poor shows contempt for their Maker; whoever gloats over disaster will not go unpunished.

PROVERBS 18:23

The poor plead for mercy, but the rich answer harshly.

PROVERBS 19:1

Better the poor whose walk is blameless than a fool whose lips are perverse.

PROVERBS 19:7

The poor are shunned by all their relatives — how much more do their friends avoid them! Though the poor pursue them with pleading, they are nowhere to be found.

PROVERBS 19:17

Whoever is kind to the poor lends to the LORD, and he will reward them for what they have done.

PROVERBS 19:22

What a person desires is unfailing love; better to be poor than a liar.

PROVERBS 21:13

Whoever shuts their ears to the cry of the poor will also cry out and not be answered.

PROVERBS 22:16

One who oppresses the poor to increase his wealth and one who gives gifts to the rich — both come to poverty.

PROVERBS 22:22–23

Do not exploit the poor because they are poor and do not crush the needy in court, for the LORD will take up their case and will exact life for life.

PROVERBS 28:6

Better the poor whose walk is blameless than the rich whose ways are perverse.

PROVERBS 28:8

Whoever increases wealth by taking interest or profit from the poor amasses it for another, who will be kind to the poor.

PROVERBS 28:11

The rich are wise in their own eyes; one who is poor and discerning sees how deluded they are.

PROVERBS 28:27

Those who give to the poor will lack nothing, but those who close their eyes to them receive many curses.

PROVERBS 29:7

The righteous care about justice for the poor, but the wicked have no such concern.

PROVERBS 31:8–9

Speak up for those who cannot speak for themselves, for the rights of all who are destitute. Speak up and judge fairly; defend the rights of the poor and needy.

_____PRAISE_____

PROVERBS 25:6

Do not exalt yourself in the king's presence, and do not claim a place among his great men.

PROVERBS 25:27

It is not good to eat too much honey, nor is it honorable to search out matters that are too deep.

PROVERBS 27:2

Let someone else praise you, and not your own mouth; an outsider, and not your own lips.

PROVERBS 27:21

The crucible for silver and the furnace for gold, but people are tested by their praise.

PROVERBS 28:4

Those who forsake instruction praise the wicked, but those who heed it resist them.

PROVERBS 31:31

Honor her for all that her hands have done, and let her works bring her praise at the city gate.

_____PRUDENCE_____

PROVERBS 8:5

"You who are simple, gain prudence; you who are foolish, set your hearts on it."

PROVERBS 12:16

Fools show their annoyance at once, but the prudent overlook an insult.

PROVERBS 12:23

The prudent keep their knowledge to themselves, but a fool's heart blurts out folly.

PROVERBS 13:16

All who are prudent act with knowledge, but fools expose their folly.

PROVERBS 14:8

The wisdom of the prudent is to give thought to their ways, but the folly of fools is deception.

PROVERBS 14:15

The simple believe anything, but the prudent give thought to their steps.

PROVERBS 14:18

The simple inherit folly, but the prudent are crowned with knowledge.

PROVERBS 15:5

A fool spurns a parent's discipline, but whoever heeds correction shows prudence.

PROVERBS 27:12

The prudent see danger and take refuge, but the simple keep going and pay the penalty.

PROVERBS 28:19

Those who work their land will have abundant food, but those who chase fantasies will have their fill of poverty.

REBUKE

PROVERBS 1:23

"Repent at my rebuke! Then I will pour out my thoughts to you, I will make known to you my teachings."

PROVERBS 1:25–26

"Since you disregard all my advice and do not accept my rebuke, I in turn will laugh when disaster strikes you; I will mock when calamity overtakes you."

PROVERBS 1:30–31

"Since they would not accept my advice and spurned my rebuke, they will eat the fruit of their ways and be filled with the fruit of their schemes."

PROVERBS 9:7–8

Whoever corrects a mocker invites insults; whoever rebukes the wicked incurs abuse. Do not rebuke mockers or they will hate you; rebuke the wise and they will love you.

PROVERBS 15:31

Whoever heeds life-giving correction will be at home among the wise.

PROVERBS 17:10

A rebuke impresses a discerning person more than a hundred lashes a fool.

PROVERBS 27:5

Better is open rebuke than hidden love.

PROVERBS 28:23

Whoever rebukes a person will in the end gain favor rather than one who has a flattering tongue.

PROVERBS 29:1

Whoever remains stiff-necked after many rebukes will suddenly be destroyed — without remedy.

REPUTATION

PROVERBS 3:4

Then you will win favor and a good name in the sight of God and man.

PROVERBS 11:16

A kindhearted woman gains honor, but ruthless men gain only wealth.

PROVERBS 20:29

The glory of young men is their strength, gray hair the splendor of the old.

PROVERBS 22:1

A good name is more desirable than great riches; to be esteemed is better than silver or gold.

PROVERBS 22:4

Humility is the fear of the LORD; its wages are riches and honor and life.

PROVERBS 22:29

Do you see someone skilled in their work? They will serve before kings; they will not serve before officials of low rank.

PROVERBS 25:9–10

If you take your neighbor to court, do not betray another's confidence, or the one who hears it may shame you and the charge against you will stand.

PROVERBS 29:23

Pride brings a person low, but the lowly in spirit gain honor.

_____REVENGE_____

PROVERBS 6:34

For jealousy arouses a husband's fury, and he will show no mercy when he takes revenge.

PROVERBS 17:5

Whoever mocks the poor shows contempt for their Maker; whoever gloats over disaster will not go unpunished.

PROVERBS 20:22

Do not say, "I'll pay you back for this wrong!" Wait for the LORD, and he will avenge you.

PROVERBS 24:17–18

Do not gloat when your enemy falls; when they stumble, do not let your heart rejoice, or the LORD will see and disapprove and turn his wrath away from them.

PROVERBS 24:29

Do not say, "I'll do to them as they have done to me; I'll pay them back for what they did."

_____RICHES_____

PROVERBS 11:4

Wealth is worthless in the day of wrath, but righteousness delivers from death.

PROVERBS 11:28

Those who trust in their riches will fall, but the righteous will thrive like a green leaf.

PROVERBS 13:7–8

One person pretends to be rich, yet has nothing; another pretends to be poor, yet has great wealth. A person's riches may ransom their life, but the poor cannot respond to threatening rebukes.

PROVERBS 13:11

Dishonest money dwindles away, but whoever gathers money little by little makes it grow.

PROVERBS 15:16

Better a little with the fear of the LORD than great wealth with turmoil.

PROVERBS 22:1

A good name is more desirable than great riches; to be esteemed is better than silver or gold.

PROVERBS 23:4–5

Do not wear yourself out to get rich; do not trust your own cleverness. Cast but a glance at riches, and they are gone, for they will surely sprout wings and fly off to the sky like an eagle.

PROVERBS 28:20

A faithful person will be richly blessed, but one eager to get rich will not go unpunished.

PROVERBS 28:22

The stingy are eager to get rich and are unaware that poverty awaits them.

_____RIGHTEOUS_____

PROVERBS 2:7

He holds success in store for the upright, he is a shield to those whose walk is blameless.

PROVERBS 4:18

The path of the righteous is like the morning sun, shining ever brighter till the full light of day.

PROVERBS 10:3

The LORD does not let the righteous go hungry, but he thwarts the craving of the wicked.

PROVERBS 10:6

Blessings crown the head of the righteous, but violence overwhelms the mouth of the wicked.

PROVERBS 10:7

The name of the righteous is used in blessings, but the name of the wicked will rot.

PROVERBS 10:9

Whoever walks in integrity walks securely, but whoever takes crooked paths will be found out.

PROVERBS 10:24–25

What the wicked dread will overtake them; what the righteous desire will be granted. When the storm has swept by, the wicked are gone, but the righteous stand firm forever.

PROVERBS 10:28–32

The prospect of the righteous is joy, but the hopes of the wicked come to nothing. The way of the LORD is a refuge for the blameless, but it is the ruin of those who do evil. The righteous will never be uprooted, but the wicked will not remain in the land. From the mouth of the righteous comes the fruit of wisdom, but a perverse tongue will be silenced. The lips of the righteous know what finds favor, but the mouth of the wicked only what is perverse.

PROVERBS 11:23

The desire of the righteous ends only in good, but the hope of the wicked only in wrath.

PROVERBS 11:30–31

The fruit of the righteous is a tree of life, and the one who is wise saves lives. If the righteous receive their due on earth, how much more the ungodly and the sinner!

PROVERBS 12:2

Good people obtain favor from the LORD, but he condemns those who devise wicked schemes.

PROVERBS 12:26

The righteous choose their friends carefully, but the way of the wicked leads them astray.

PROVERBS 13:5

The righteous hate what is false, but the wicked make themselves a stench and bring shame on themselves.

PROVERBS 15:28–29

The heart of the righteous weighs its answers, but the mouth of the wicked gushes evil. The LORD is far from the wicked, but he hears the prayer of the righteous.

PROVERBS 18:10

The name of the LORD is a fortified tower; the righteous run to it and are safe.

PROVERBS 20:7

The righteous lead blameless lives; blessed are their children after them.

PROVERBS 21:26

All day long he craves for more, but the righteous give without sparing.

PROVERBS 24:16

For though the righteous fall seven times, they rise again, but the wicked stumble when calamity strikes.

PROVERBS 28:1

The wicked flee though no one pursues, but the righteous are as bold as a lion.

_____RIGHTEOUSNESS_____

PROVERBS 11:4–6

Wealth is worthless in the day of wrath, but righteousness delivers from death. The righteousness of the blameless makes their paths straight, but the wicked are brought down by their own wickedness. The righteousness of the upright delivers them, but the unfaithful are trapped by evil desires.

PROVERBS 11:18

A wicked person earns deceptive wages, but the one who sows righteousness reaps a sure reward.

PROVERBS 12:28

In the way of righteousness there is life; along that path is immortality.

PROVERBS 13:6

Righteousness guards the person of integrity, but wickedness overthrows the sinner.

PROVERBS 14:34

Righteousness exalts a nation, but sin condemns any people.

PROVERBS 15:9

The LORD detests the way of the wicked, but he loves those who pursue righteousness.

PROVERBS 16:8

Better a little with righteousness than much gain with injustice.

PROVERBS 16:12

Kings detest wrongdoing, for a throne is established through righteousness.

_____SELF-CONTROL_____

PROVERBS 15:18

A hot-tempered person stirs up conflict, but the one who is patient calms a quarrel.

PROVERBS 15:32

Those who disregard discipline despise themselves, but the one who heeds correction gains understanding.

PROVERBS 16:32

Better a patient person than a warrior, one with self-control than one who takes a city.

PROVERBS 17:27

The one who has knowledge uses words with restraint, and whoever has understanding is even-tempered.

PROVERBS 23:1–4

When you sit to dine with a ruler, note well what is before you, and put a knife to your throat if you are given to gluttony. Do not crave his delicacies, for that food is deceptive. Do not wear yourself out to get rich; do not trust your own cleverness.

PROVERBS 23:20–21

Do not join those who drink too much wine or gorge themselves on meat, for drunkards and gluttons become poor, and drowsiness clothes them in rags.

PROVERBS 25:16

If you find honey, eat just enough — too much of it, and you will vomit.

PROVERBS 25:28

Like a city whose walls are broken through is a person who lacks self-control.

_____SIMPLE_____

PROVERBS 1:22

"How long will you who are simple love your simple ways? How long will mockers delight in mockery and fools hate knowledge?"

PROVERBS 1:32

"For the waywardness of the simple will kill them, and the complacency of fools will destroy them."

PROVERBS 8:5

"You who are simple, gain prudence; you who are foolish, set your hearts on it."

PROVERBS 9:6

"Leave your simple ways and you will live; walk in the way of insight."

PROVERBS 14:15

The simple believe anything, but the prudent give thought to their steps.

PROVERBS 14:18

The simple inherit folly, but the prudent are crowned with knowledge.

PROVERBS 19:25

Flog a mocker, and the simple will learn prudence; rebuke the discerning, and they will gain knowledge.

PROVERBS 21:11

When a mocker is punished, the simple gain wisdom; by paying attention to the wise they get knowledge.

PROVERBS 22:3

The prudent see danger and take refuge, but the simple keep going and pay the penalty.

PROVERBS 27:12

The prudent see danger and take refuge, but the simple keep going and pay the penalty.

_____SLANDER/GOSSIP_____

PROVERBS 10:18

Whoever conceals hatred with lying lips and spreads slander is a fool.

PROVERBS 11:13

A gossip betrays a confidence, but a trustworthy person keeps a secret.

PROVERBS 16:28

A perverse person stirs up conflict, and a gossip separates close friends.

PROVERBS 18:8

The words of a gossip are like choice morsels; they go down to the inmost parts.

PROVERBS 20:19

A gossip betrays a confidence; so avoid anyone who talks too much.

PROVERBS 26:20

Without wood a fire goes out; without a gossip a quarrel dies down.

PROVERBS 30:10

"Do not slander a servant to their master, or they will curse you, and you will pay for it."

_____SON, FOOLISH_____

PROVERBS 10:5

He who gathers crops in summer is a prudent son, but he who sleeps during harvest is a disgraceful son.

PROVERBS 15:5

A fool spurns a parent's discipline, but whoever heeds correction shows prudence.

PROVERBS 15:20

A wise son brings joy to his father, but a foolish man despises his mother.

PROVERBS 19:13

A foolish child is a father's ruin, and a quarrelsome wife is like the constant dripping of a leaky roof.

PROVERBS 19:26

Whoever robs their father and drives out their mother is a child who brings shame and disgrace.

PROVERBS 20:20

If someone curses their father or mother, their lamp will be snuffed out in pitch darkness.

PROVERBS 28:7

A discerning son heeds instruction, but a companion of gluttons disgraces his father.

PROVERBS 28:24

Whoever robs their father or mother and says, "It's not wrong," is partner to one who destroys.

PROVERBS 30:17

"The eye that mocks a father, that scorns an aged mother, will be pecked out by the ravens of the valley, will be eaten by the vultures."

_____SON, WISE_____

PROVERBS 2:1–5

My son, if you accept my words and store up my commands within you, turning your ear to wisdom and applying your heart to understanding — indeed, if you call out for insight and cry aloud for understanding, and if you look for it as for silver and search for it as for hidden treasure, then you will understand the fear of the LORD and find the knowledge of God.

PROVERBS 3:21–24

My son, do not let wisdom and understanding out of your sight, preserve sound judgment and discretion; they will be life for you, an ornament to grace your neck. Then you will go on your way in safety, and your foot will not stumble. When you lie down, you will not be afraid; when you lie down, your sleep will be sweet.

PROVERBS 4:10–12

Listen, my son, accept what I say, and the years of your life will be many. I instruct you in the way of wisdom and lead you along straight paths. When you walk, your steps will not be hampered; when you run, you will not stumble.

PROVERBS 5:1–2

My son, pay attention to my wisdom, turn your ear to my words of insight, that you may maintain discretion and your lips may preserve knowledge.

_____SPEECH_____

PROVERBS 10:11

The mouth of the righteous is a fountain of life, but the mouth of the wicked conceals violence.

PROVERBS 10:19–21

Sin is not ended by multiplying words, but the prudent hold their tongues. The tongue of the righteous is choice silver, but the heart of the wicked is of little value. The lips of the righteous nourish many, but fools die for lack of sense.

PROVERBS 10:31–32

From the mouth of the righteous comes the fruit of wisdom, but a perverse tongue will be silenced. The lips of the righteous know what finds favor, but the mouth of the wicked only what is perverse.

PROVERBS 12:6

The words of the wicked lie in wait for blood, but the speech of the upright rescues them.

PROVERBS 12:14

From the fruit of their lips people are filled with good things, and the work of their hands brings them reward.

PROVERBS 12:18–19

The words of the reckless pierce like swords, but the tongue of the wise brings healing. Truthful lips endure forever, but a lying tongue lasts only a moment.

PROVERBS 12:25

Anxiety weighs down the heart, but a kind word cheers it up.

PROVERBS 13:3

Those who guard their lips preserve their lives, but those who speak rashly will come to ruin.

PROVERBS 15:1–2

A gentle answer turns away wrath, but a harsh word stirs up anger. The tongue of the wise adorns knowledge, but the mouth of the fool gushes folly.

PROVERBS 15:4

The soothing tongue is a tree of life, but a perverse tongue crushes the spirit.

PROVERBS 15:23

A person finds joy in giving an apt reply — and how good is a timely word!

PROVERBS 15:28

The heart of the righteous weighs its answers, but the mouth of the wicked gushes evil.

PROVERBS 16:23–24

The hearts of the wise make their mouths prudent, and their lips promote instruction. Gracious words are a honeycomb, sweet to the soul and healing to the bones.

PROVERBS 17:14

Starting a quarrel is like breaching a dam; so drop the matter before a dispute breaks out.

PROVERBS 17:27

The one who has knowledge uses words with restraint, and whoever has understanding is even-tempered.

PROVERBS 18:20–21

From the fruit of their mouth a person's stomach is filled; with the harvest of their lips they are satisfied. The tongue has the power of life and death, and those who love it will eat its fruit.

PROVERBS 20:19

A gossip betrays a confidence; so avoid anyone who talks too much.

PROVERBS 21:23

Those who guard their mouths and their tongues keep themselves from calamity.

PROVERBS 25:11

Like apples of gold in settings of silver is a ruling rightly given.

PROVERBS 25:15

Through patience a ruler can be persuaded, and a gentle tongue can break a bone.

PROVERBS 26:17–19

Like one who grabs a stray dog by the ears is someone who rushes into a quarrel not their own. Like a maniac shooting flaming arrows of death is one who deceives their neighbor and says, "I was only joking!"

PROVERBS 26:21–25

As charcoal to embers and as wood to fire, so is a quarrelsome person for kindling strife. The words of a gossip are like choice morsels; they go down to the inmost parts. Like a coating of silver dross on earthenware are fervent lips with an evil heart. Enemies disguise themselves with their lips, but in their hearts they harbor deceit. Though their speech is charming, do not believe them, for seven abominations fill their hearts.

PROVERBS 27:2

Let someone else praise you, and not your own mouth; an outsider, and not your own lips.

PROVERBS 30:32

"If you play the fool and exalt yourself, or if you plan evil, clap your hand over your mouth!"

_____SPIRIT_____

PROVERBS 15:4

The soothing tongue is a tree of life, but a perverse tongue crushes the spirit.

PROVERBS 15:13

A happy heart makes the face cheerful, but heartache crushes the spirit.

PROVERBS 16:18–19

Pride goes before destruction, a haughty spirit before a fall. Better to be lowly in spirit along with the oppressed than to share plunder with the proud.

PROVERBS 17:22

A cheerful heart is good medicine, but a crushed spirit dries up the bones.

PROVERBS 18:14

The human spirit can endure in sickness, but a crushed spirit who can bear?

PROVERBS 20:27

The human spirit is the lamp of the LORD that sheds light on one's inmost being.

PROVERBS 25:13

Like a snow-cooled drink at harvest time is a trustworthy messenger to the one who sends him; he refreshes the spirit of his master.

PROVERBS 29:23

Pride brings a person low, but the lowly in spirit gain honor.

STRIFE

PROVERBS 6:12–15

A troublemaker and a villain, who goes about with a corrupt mouth, who winks maliciously with his eye, signals with his feet and motions with his fingers, who plots evil with deceit in his heart — he always stirs up conflict. Therefore disaster will overtake him in an instant; he will suddenly be destroyed — without remedy.

PROVERBS 10:12

Hatred stirs up conflict, but love covers over all wrongs.

PROVERBS 13:10

Where there is strife, there is pride, but wisdom is found in those who take advice.

PROVERBS 15:18

A hot-tempered person stirs up conflict, but the one who is patient calms a quarrel.

PROVERBS 17:14

Starting a quarrel is like breaching a dam; so drop the matter before a dispute breaks out.

PROVERBS 17:19

Whoever loves a quarrel loves sin; whoever builds a high gate invites destruction.

PROVERBS 20:3

It is to one's honor to avoid strife, but every fool is quick to quarrel.

PROVERBS 22:24

Do not make friends with a hot-tempered person, do not associate with one easily angered.

PROVERBS 26:20–21

Without wood a fire goes out; without a gossip a quarrel dies down. As charcoal to embers and as wood to fire, so is a quarrelsome person for kindling strife.

_____UNDERSTANDING_____

PROVERBS 9:6

"Leave your simple ways and you will live; walk in the way of insight."

PROVERBS 9:10

The fear of the LORD is the beginning of wisdom, and knowledge of the Holy One is understanding.

PROVERBS 11:12

Whoever derides their neighbor has no sense, but the one who has understanding holds their tongue.

PROVERBS 13:15

Good judgment wins favor, but the way of the unfaithful leads to their destruction.

PROVERBS 15:21

Folly brings joy to one who has no sense, but whoever has understanding keeps a straight course.

PROVERBS 15:32

Those who disregard discipline despise themselves, but the one who heeds correction gains understanding.

PROVERBS 16:22

Prudence is a fountain of life to the prudent, but folly brings punishment to fools.

PROVERBS 20:5

The purposes of a person's heart are deep waters, but one who has insight draws them out.

PROVERBS 28:2

When a country is rebellious, it has many rulers, but a ruler with discernment and knowledge maintains order.

PROVERBS 28:5

Evildoers do not understand what is right, but those who seek the LORD understand it fully.

_____VIOLENCE_____

PROVERBS 3:31

Do not envy the violent or choose any of their ways.

PROVERBS 4:17

They eat the bread of wickedness and drink the wine of violence.

PROVERBS 10:6

Blessings crown the head of the righteous, but violence overwhelms the mouth of the wicked.

PROVERBS 10:11

The mouth of the righteous is a fountain of life, but the mouth of the wicked conceals violence.

PROVERBS 13:2

From the fruit of their lips people enjoy good things, but the unfaithful have an appetite for violence.

PROVERBS 16:29

A violent person entices their neighbor and leads them down a path that is not good.

PROVERBS 21:7

The violence of the wicked will drag them away, for they refuse to do what is right.

PROVERBS 24:2

For their hearts plot violence, and their lips talk about making trouble.

PROVERBS 26:6

Sending a message by the hands of a fool is like cutting off one's feet or drinking poison.

WISDOM

PROVERBS 1:7

The fear of the LORD is the beginning of knowledge, but fools despise wisdom and instruction.

PROVERBS 2:1–6

My son, if you accept my words and store up my commands within you, turning your ear to wisdom and applying your heart to understanding — indeed, if you call out for insight and cry aloud for understanding, and if you look for it as for silver and search for it as for hidden treasure, then you will understand the fear of the LORD and find the knowledge of God. For the LORD gives wisdom; from his mouth come knowledge and understanding.

PROVERBS 2:10–22

For wisdom will enter your heart, and knowledge will be pleasant to your soul. Discretion will protect you, and understanding will guard you. Wisdom will save you from the ways of wicked men, from men whose words are perverse, who have left the straight paths to walk in dark ways, who delight in doing wrong and rejoice in the perverseness of evil, whose paths are crooked and who are devious in their ways. Wisdom will save you also from the adulterous woman, from the wayward woman with her seductive words, who has left the partner of her youth and ignored the covenant she made before God. Surely her house leads down to death and her paths to the spirits of the dead. None who go to her return or attain the paths of life. Thus you will walk in the ways of the good and keep to the paths of the righteous. For the upright will live in the land, and the blameless will remain in it; but the wicked will be cut off from the land, and the unfaithful will be torn from it.

PROVERBS 3:13–19

Blessed are those who find wisdom, those who gain understanding, for she is more profitable than silver and yields better returns than gold. She is more precious than rubies; nothing you desire can compare with her. Long life is in her right hand; in her left hand are riches and honor. Her ways are pleasant ways, and all her paths are peace. She is a tree of life to those who take hold of her; those who hold her fast will be blessed. By wisdom the LORD laid the earth's foundations, by understanding he set the heavens in place.

PROVERBS 4:5–11

"Get wisdom, get understanding; do not forget my words or turn away from them. Do not forsake wisdom, and she will protect you; love her, and she will watch over you. The beginning of wisdom is this: Get wisdom. Though it cost all you have, get understanding. Cherish her, and she will exalt you; embrace her, and she will honor you. She will give you a garland to grace your head and present you with a glorious crown." Listen, my son, accept what I say, and the years of your life will be many. I instruct you in the way of wisdom and lead you along straight paths.

PROVERBS 8:11

For wisdom is more precious than rubies, and nothing you desire can compare with her.

PROVERBS 10:13

Wisdom is found on the lips of the discerning, but a rod is for the back of one who has no sense.

PROVERBS 10:23

A fool finds pleasure in wicked schemes, but a person of understanding delights in wisdom.

PROVERBS 10:31

From the mouth of the righteous comes the fruit of wisdom, but a perverse tongue will be silenced.

PROVERBS 11:2

When pride comes, then comes disgrace, but with humility comes wisdom.

PROVERBS 12:8

A person is praised according to their prudence, and one with a warped mind is despised.

PROVERBS 13:10

Where there is strife, there is pride, but wisdom is found in those who take advice.

PROVERBS 14:6

The mocker seeks wisdom and finds none, but knowledge comes easily to the discerning.

PROVERBS 14:8

The wisdom of the prudent is to give thought to their ways, but the folly of fools is deception.

PROVERBS 14:33

Wisdom reposes in the heart of the discerning and even among fools she lets herself be known.

PROVERBS 15:33

Wisdom's instruction is to fear the LORD, and humility comes before honor.

PROVERBS 16:16

How much better to get wisdom than gold, to get insight rather than silver!

PROVERBS 17:24

A discerning person keeps wisdom in view, but a fool's eyes wander to the ends of the earth.

PROVERBS 18:4

The words of the mouth are deep waters, but the fountain of wisdom is a rushing stream.

PROVERBS 19:8

The one who gets wisdom loves life; the one who cherishes understanding will soon prosper.

PROVERBS 19:11

A person's wisdom yields patience; it is to one's glory to overlook an offense.

PROVERBS 21:11

When a mocker is punished, the simple gain wisdom; by paying attention to the wise they get knowledge.

PROVERBS 21:30

There is no wisdom, no insight, no plan that can succeed against the LORD.

PROVERBS 23:4

Do not wear yourself out to get rich; do not trust your own cleverness.

PROVERBS 23:23

Buy the truth and do not sell it — wisdom, instruction and insight as well.